Christmas 2010

To: _Mary_____

From: _Shannon_____

Other books by Gregory E. Lang:

Why a Daughter Needs a Dad

Why a Daughter Needs a Mom

Why a Son Needs a Mom

Why a Son Needs a Dad

Why I Love Grandma

Why I Love Grandpa

Why I Chose You

Why I Still Love You

Why I Need You

Why We Are a Family

Why We Are Friends

Brothers and Sisters

Simple Acts

Love Signs

Life Maps

Thank You, Mom

Thank You, Dad

Why I Love You

· 100 Reasons ·

GREGORY E. LANG

CUMBERLAND HOUSE

AN IMPRINT OF SOURCEBOOKS, INC.®

Copyright © 2004 by Gregory E. Lang
Cover design: JulesRulesDesign
Text design: Lisa Taylor
Photographs: Gregory E. Lang

Published by Cumberland House Publishing, an imprint of Sourcebooks, Inc.
P.O. Box 4410, Naperville, Illinois 60567–4410
(630) 961–3900
Fax: (630) 961–2168
www.sourcebooks.com

Printed and bound in the United States of America.
LB 10 9 8 7 6 5 4 3 2

To Jill:
You love my heart, for once it was your own,
And I cherish yours, because in me it now resides.
I am yours, irreversibly.

Introduction

One of life's great experiences is falling in love so deeply one cannot imagine ever being without the other. Whether a first love, a new love, or a rekindled love, we universally experience the wonderful feelings that come when we find that special person—the intense feelings of attachment, the euphoric passion, the promise of a happy future together. Some of us find one true love and keep that partner for a lifetime. Others have love that eventually fades, but remain ever hopeful of finding a new and longer-lasting love one day. Some have not yet fallen in love and are searching for the person that will fulfill their romantic dreams. No matter where we are in our lives or what else may occupy our time, we all wish to have someone to love, someone who will love us in return.

When it comes to falling in love there are, I think, two kinds of people. The first is one who has a well-laid plan by which they seek a partner that possesses certain preferred qualities and characteristics. Upon finding such a person, they pursue a cautious and measured courtship, waiting for signs of reassurance before giving in to feelings of attachment, never taking too much risk, slowly and incrementally revealing more about themselves, until a respectable time has passed and a sense of comfort has been attained, before ever coming near uttering those three powerful words, "I love you."

The second kind has no such plan or patience for caution. They will think nothing of the risk being taken when investing in someone, nor will they bother to proceed carefully, but will choose instead to reveal everything about themselves to whomever wishes to know them. These are the people who believe in serendipity, who trust their feelings and are led by their heart, who are on a relentless quest to find, earn, and keep love in their lives. These are the people who do not tiptoe into love, but instead know only to dive in, head first, with abandon. I am one of these people.

Exhilarated by the dive, I like it when my heart pounds so fast and strong that I can feel it in my chest and hear it in my ears. I enjoy the hope that swells inside, and I look forward to discovering what promise the relationship may hold. I don't stop to think about what I am doing, but instead choose to feel my way along, not knowing if it will last but trusting that I will gain something worthwhile from the experience, giving of myself what I can and hoping for my affections to be returned. Sometimes I have been rewarded, and other times not. Sometimes I have been disappointed and hurt. Sometimes, regrettably, I have done the disappointing and hurting. Yet, through it all, I have continued to approach relationships in the same way, head first, without hesitation, hoping each time to find the relationship from which a *lasting* love would grow.

I have been in love more than once. Although at times I have been heartbroken, I have few regrets about these failed relationships because each of them, from high school infatuations to relationships of my adulthood, has fulfilled a special need in my life at the time, helping me to discover more about myself and improving my understanding of intimacy and commitment. For me, each relationship has been another step in the journey to a more meaningful capacity to truly love someone. I have learned much along the way.

I have learned that love is like a diamond, hard and durable, yet if handled carelessly, can cleave into worthless fragments. A relationship must be cared for and nourished if it is to remain whole. Care and nourishment may take many forms, like sending love letters, bringing home flowers, or planning romantic evenings together. Care and nourishment can also be simple, like speaking from one's heart and telling the other of the love that is inspired within you. I have learned that love involves risk, and it is only after taking risk and finding that no harm will come that a deeper love can grow. I have learned that love involves work. It brings with it challenges and compromises, and it sometimes brings tears, but with the desire to carry out one's commitment with passion and persistence, it is work worth doing and even more love is the reward. Above all, I think the most valuable lesson I have learned is that love cannot go unexpressed. Signs of love must be demonstrated and words of love must be spoken if love is to continuously flow with vigor. It is this lesson that has brought me to write this book.

Recently and unexpectedly a great and wonderful blessing was visited upon me, and the next time—the last time—has come. I have met a woman, a woman who reminds me each day why I enjoy being in love, a woman who is teaching me more about loving than I have ever known. She gives me acceptance, kindness, and grace that compel me to better myself for her enjoyment. She pleases all my senses, stimulates my mind and my passions, and encourages my ever-increasing hunger for her company. She lets me love her the way I want to, and welcomes all that I have to give her. She tirelessly shows her love and enthusiasm for me. I have told her of my many weaknesses and trespasses, and she has not retreated from me. I have revealed to her my fears, and she has comforted me. I do not know how I became so fortunate, but I know that I am.

It is because of this woman that I, for the first time, now question myself and my past relationships, worrying that the way in which I have conducted myself leaves me suspect when I tell her how I feel about her. What if I cannot adequately express to her what she has come to mean to me, or why she is different from those I have known before her? I worry that I'll be unable to say something original to her or do something for the first time with her to make it clear to her and to others that *this time* it is different. Out of this worry comes a determination and resolve to do the only thing I know how to do, but to do it better than ever before, and that is, to just dive in. So it is with this book that I fearlessly walk to the edge and declare that I want to be with her—now and always. When I first place it in her hands, it will be with this book that I tell her, "I love you, and I want to tell you why."

WHY I LOVE YOU

I love you because

you kiss me like you mean it.

I love you because

when your arms fold around me,
all my worries disappear.

I love you because . . .

you find a way to make me feel special each and every day.

you never tire of my need
for your attention.

you have never been indifferent to my love for you.

I love you because . . .

you always smile when our eyes meet.

you are proud to be seen with me.

you help me without me having to ask.

I love you because

time has shown me that I can trust you.

I love you because . . .

you don't demand more of me than I can give you.

you have always kept my secrets.

you get sentimental when looking at our old photographs.

I love you because

when I am irritable, you are forgiving.

I love you because . . .

you honor my family traditions.

you always give me the benefit of the doubt.

you know what I meant to say, even if I didn't say it.

I love you because

you have never betrayed my trust in you.

I love you because . . .

you don't expect me to be everything to you.

when I want to talk, you listen.

when I do not want to talk, you are patient.

you give me the freedom to take care of others
in my life who are important to me.

I love you because

you indulge my romantic impulses.

I love you because . . .

you have never caused me heartache.

you never fail to consider my feelings.

you like to sleep like spoons.

I love you because

when I want to admire you,
you do not shy away from me.

I love you because

even though time has changed me,
you still find me attractive.

I love you because

I know without a doubt that you love me, too.

I love you because

it is important to you that I am happy.

I love you because . . . .

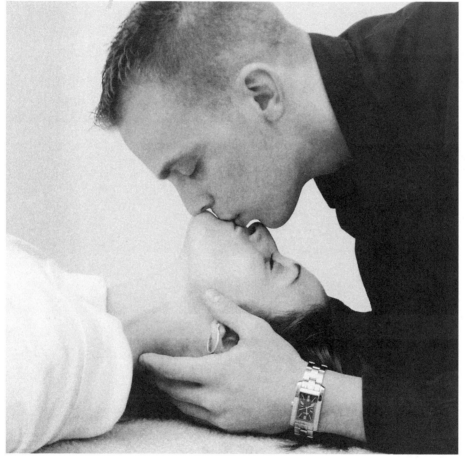

you have given all of yourself to me.

*you accept all the affection
I want to give you.*

you continue to surprise me.

I love you because . . .

you encourage me in all that I do.

you can always tell when I need a hug.

when I touch you, you touch me back.

you are as crazy about me as I am about you.

I love you because

you have never looked back
at what came before me.

I love you because

you kiss me when you think I am asleep.

I love you because

when I reach for you, you move closer.

I love you because

when I need you, you drop everything to comfort me.

I love you because . . .

you have shown me grace at my every wrong turn.

you have helped me to better understand myself.

you have never tried to change who I am.

when I gave myself to you, I lost nothing.

I love you because

you have enriched my life in ways I never imagined.

I love you because

you are careful with my tender spots.

I love you because

you are not afraid of commitment.

I love you because . . .

you have never stopped courting me.

you surprise me with little gifts.

you dance with me whenever I ask.

you have saved everything I have ever given you.

I love you because

I always have fun with you.

I love you because

you try to seduce me when you think no one is watching.

I love you because

I feel safe with you.

I love you because

you always see the best in me.

I love you because . . .

you have never asked me to prove myself to you.

even when we are apart, you think of me.

you carry a picture of me everywhere you go.

you are always prepared to defend me.

I love you because

you know how to turn around a bad day.

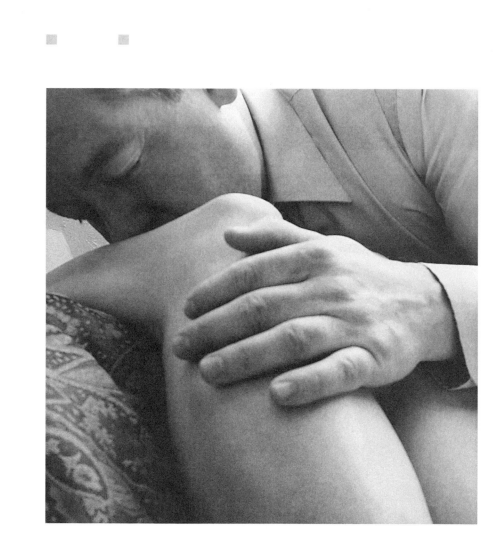

I love you because

you take your time with me.

I love you because

you still treat me like you did when we were first dating.

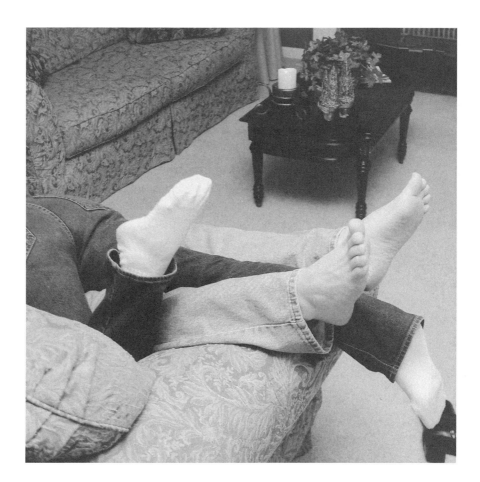

I love you because

your desire for me is unfettered.

I love you because

you cherish each moment we spend together.

I love you because

you find me irresistible.

I love you because . . .

when we spend time together you are never distracted

by something more important.

with you I have a profound
sense of belonging.

you understand my needs.

I love you because

I can feel your heart when you touch me.

I love you because

you are my best friend.

I love you because . . .

you accept my family as your own.

you put our relationship above all others.

you tell me what you need from me.

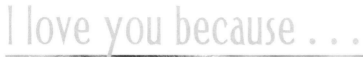
I love you because . . .

you know how to say the difficult things

without hurting my feelings.

when I look into your eyes,
I see your love for me.

you always embrace me when you see me.

I love you because

your compliments are always sincere.

I love you because

we made a family together.

I love you because . . .

you still chase me around the house.

you are faithful to our promises to each other.

you know all the words to our song.

I love you because

you never grow tired of hearing me say, "I love you."

I love you because

you reserve private time for us.

I love you because . . .

even when you are angry with me, you are kind.

you never attempt to control me.

you do not put yourself in situations that would

make me uncomfortable.

I love you because

we strive equally for harmony in our relationship.

I love you because

you always forgive me.

I love you because

you are devoted to me.

I love you because

you share my faith and values.

I love you because . . .

I can lean on you when I am weak.

you love me for who I am.

you still write me love letters.

I love you because

your lips are always eager to meet mine.

I love you because

your affection soothes me.

I love you because . . .

we made a home together.

you like to spoil me now and then.

you are proud of my accomplishments.

when I can't sleep, you rub my back.

I love you because

without you my life would be less
than it has become.

Acknowledgments

This book could not have been written without the trust and openness of many couples. I offer a heartfelt thanks to the men and women who shared their love stories with me, who overcame their modesty in order to let me capture intimate moments in photographs, and who helped me stay true to the vision of this book—that there really is one special person out there for each of us. I was deeply touched by the sincerity I witnessed in the time I spent with all of you.

I also wish to thank Ron Pitkin, my publisher, and the staff at Cumberland House, including my editor, Lisa Taylor, who once more helped me to make this book the best it could be. Ron, I appreciate so much your confidence in me and the investment you have made in furthering my writing career. Julie Jayne, Stacie and Chris Bauerle, and Teresa Wright, thank you all.

Finally, I want to thank my dear friend of more than thirty years, Patricia DeBary, who introduced me to Jill. Thanks, hon; what a marvelous favor you have done for me.

To Contact the Author

write in care of the publisher:
Cumberland House Publishing/Sourcebooks, Inc.
P.O. Box 4410
Naperville, IL 60567-4410

e-mail the author or visit his Web site:
greg.lang@mindspring.com
www. gregoryelang.com